The Care & Keeping of YOU 2

The Body Book for Older Girls

by Dr. Cara Natterson

illustrated by Josée Masse

⭐ American Girl®

Published by American Girl Publishing
Copyright © 2012 by American Girl

Questions or comments? Call 1-800-845-0005, visit **americangirl.com**, or write to Customer Service, American Girl, 8400 Fairway Place, Middleton, WI 53562-0497.

Printed in China
12 13 14 15 16 17 18 19 20 LEO 10 9 8 7 6 5 4 3 2 1

Editorial Development: Carrie Anton, Mary Richards, Barbara Stretchberry
Art Direction and Design: Camela Decaire
Production: Judith Lary, Sarah Boecher, Tami Kepler, Jeannette Bailey
Illustrations: Josée Masse

This book is not intended to replace the advice or treatment of health-care professionals. It should be considered an additional resource only. Questions and concerns about mental or physical health should always be discussed with a doctor or other health-care professional.

07 13

Letter to You

Dear Reader,

As you are getting older, everything about you is changing: the way you look, the way you are shaped, the way you feel, the way you react, and the things that you find interesting. This happens for every girl your age, but sometimes it feels as if you are the only one going through it.

This book will help you realize that the changes are a normal part of growing up. Starting where *The Care and Keeping of You* leaves off, this guide has even more information about your changing body so that you understand what's going on. And then it explains your changing brain, your changing feelings, and your changing world. Each of these is a part of going through puberty. Most of the changes you see in yourself are normal, but they may not always feel that way to you. Reading and learning more about them really helps.

Most important, this book will teach you how to ask questions when you are worried. Your parents are there for you, and so are other trusted adults, such as doctors and family members. Just remember that they all went through puberty, too, so they probably have the answers to your questions. If they don't, they can help you find the answers.

You are growing and changing. This book will help you understand those changes and continue to celebrate you!

Your friends at American Girl

Contents

Back to Body Basics

Throughout puberty, your body will change shape, getting taller and curvier. In order for you to grow your best, it's important that you take extra care by eating right, keeping clean, and getting sleep. This section reminds you about body basics to keep you looking and feeling your best.

Treat Your Body Right

Respect yourself! Your body is the only one you'll ever have.

Even though ice cream is a dairy product, it has so much sugar that it really isn't a healthy source of calcium or protein—it counts as a treat instead.

Growing a Healthy You

Being healthy depends upon what you put into—and keep out of—your body. One of the ways you can help your body grow best is by eating a balanced diet of nutritious foods. Now's the time to make sure to get a variety of vitamins and minerals in your food. And two of the most important body builders are calcium and protein.

Calcium is a mineral that helps make your bones strong. Calcium also strengthens your teeth, powers your nerves, and keeps your blood and heart healthy. You can find calcium in foods such as these:
- dairy products: milk, cheese, and yogurt
- dark green leafy vegetables
- beans: white, black, kidney, and garbanzo
- orange-colored fruits: cantaloupes, tangerines, and oranges
- fish, particularly salmon
- calcium-fortified foods such as orange juice and cereals (look for "calcium-fortified" on the label)

Protein is needed to keep up and build the muscles you use every day. Lean meats and fish have lots of protein without a lot of unhealthy fats. But if you're not much of a meat eater or if you're a vegetarian, here are some great alternatives:
- beans (combine beans with rice for even more protein)
- dairy products: milk, cheese, and yogurt
- soy: soybeans/edamame and tofu
- nuts and nut butters
- eggs

Listen to Your Body

What's important is not only what you eat but also how often and how much you eat. Many people eat three large meals a day—breakfast, lunch, and dinner—but it's actually better to eat five smaller meals. If you eat a snack in the morning, a snack in the afternoon, and reasonable portions at breakfast, lunch, and dinner, then you are already doing it!

Don't forget to pace yourself. Listen to your body, eating when you are hungry and stopping when you are full. If you eat extremely fast, you won't always feel full until you've already eaten too much food. But don't go too slowly either, or you won't have time to finish lunch at school!

Meal Skipping

Skipping meals typically isn't a good idea. If you're sick, your body might not feel as if it wants solid food, so drinking water, tea, juice, or soup is fine. But in general, your body needs food regularly.

The saying "breakfast is the most important meal of the day" is actually true! That's because breakfast provides the fuel to start your day—it gives your body and your brain the energy to get going. Even if you don't feel hungry, it's a bad idea to skip breakfast. If you do skip it, you may not have the energy to do well in your early classes and may be so hungry by lunchtime that you make bad food choices.

The Real Thing Is Best

A meal with whole foods is the best way to get good nutrition into your body—this means eating unprocessed foods, such as fresh fruit instead of fruit gummies, or cheese, yogurt, meat, or beans instead of a protein bar. You might think you can just take a vitamin to make your diet a healthy one, but that doesn't work, because your body absorbs nutrients much better from whole foods than from a pill.

Foods That Can Fool You

Respecting your body is as much about keeping bad things out of it as it is about putting good things in. Junk food doesn't help you grow in a healthy way, and it sometimes leaves you feeling tired or can lead to stomach aches. Some junk foods are obvious: candy, cakes, ice cream, sodas, and fried foods (such as chips and French fries). But the ones that can fool you are usually drinks!

A vitamin-enriched water or sports drink is usually packed with sugars, artificial flavorings, and fake colors. It adds calories to your body without bringing any nutrition. Unless you are an elite athlete, you don't need a sports drink after a game—water is better. Some of these drinks also have *caffeine*, a chemical that can keep you up at night or interrupt your sleep, potentially making you moody and slowing your growth.

Even though you might know which foods aren't good for you, cravings still creep up. The best rule is to keep junk foods to a minimum. This means that if you have already eaten something junky, you should be done with treats for the day. And when you choose a food that you know isn't great for you, eat a reasonable amount and don't overdo it!

In addition to junk food, it's also important to stay away from cigarettes, alcohol, and drugs. Each can hurt your body in different ways and can make you think unclearly or act foolishly. If your doctor gives you a prescription medicine, it is meant for you and only you—don't ever offer your medicine to someone else, and don't take someone else's medicine yourself.

When in Doubt, Keep It Out!

When you walk through the grocery store or pharmacy, you will see lots of different vitamins and supplements promising all sorts of results. The bottle may say, "Take this and lose weight!" or "Build strong muscles!" Or the label may have a picture of a person who looks the way you would like to look. Don't believe everything that is advertised! Many of these products won't do what they say they will. Even worse, some are dangerous to a growing, changing body like yours. Talk to your parents and a doctor about what supplements are safe and healthy for your body. And when in doubt, keep it out!

Your New Look

As your body matures, get ready to grow in different directions.

Figure Facts

You may start to notice new curves where you never had them—particularly around your thighs, hips, waist, and breasts. Your body may look bigger than it used to, or your pants may feel tighter in some places. All of these changes are normal. But curves aren't required! It's common for your body to begin to look more like the bodies of other women in your family. So if your mom is long, lean, and less curvy, you might shape up the same way.

Body shapes are meant to be different, and just because you're developing faster than your friend is or slower than your older sister did doesn't mean there is anything wrong with you. Girls can grow tall before they gain weight, or they can gain weight before they grow tall.

In most cases, in order to grow into a taller, healthy teenager, you need to gain weight. And to gain weight, you need to increase the amount of food you eat. That's because it takes a lot of energy for your body to stretch and grow, and food provides this fuel. Sometimes girls are nervous about gaining weight, thinking that it means they are becoming overweight and unhealthy. But the truth is that healthy weight gain is normal and important.

Good Growing

Your doctor will weigh and measure you each year and will let you know whether or not you are gaining at the right pace for you. To do this, your doctor will use a mathematical equation called *body mass index,* or *BMI,* which bases your weight on your height.

You don't need to worry about doing the math; that's the doctor's job. The most important lesson is to know that when it comes to your weight, you're not alone. If your doctor has concerns—if your weight is too low or too high—then you will work together with your doctor and your parents to make a healthy plan. It's usually not necessary to check your weight at home, and for this reason most doctors recommend that families get rid of their scales.

Reaching New Heights

Get ready to grow!

Sample equation:
If your mom is 5'3"
and your dad is 5'10",
then you would do
the following math:
5'3" = 63"; 5'10" = 70"

70	65	128
− 5	+63	÷ 2
65"	128"	64"

64" = 5'4", your estimated
height, give or take 2".

Ready, Set, Grow!

Since toddler age, you've grown about two inches every year. But at some point, usually around age 9 or 10, you'll enter a growth spurt and grow faster than ever before. The average girl grows three and a half inches per year during this time. And whether it happens earlier or later during *puberty* (the time when the body begins to develop and change), it almost always lasts about two to three years.

But your body may grow in unpredictable ways. You could grow fast when you're young, and then stop growing before other girls even begin their growth spurts, making you the tallest girl in elementary school but one of the shorter girls in high school. Or maybe you'll have your growth spurt much later, surprising friends in high school by winding up as the tallest teenager when you started out on the small side. Girls can start tall and stay tall or start small and stay small, too.

How Will You Measure Up?

Only time will tell how tall you'll be, but with a bit of math you can try to predict your future. To do so, take your dad's height in inches and subtract five (that's how tall he might have been if he had been a girl). Then add your mom's height in inches and divide the total number by two. This is your *mid-parental height*. Body height isn't an exact science, so there is a pretty good chance that you will be around that height, give or take two inches—but no guarantee.

(Note: The math is different for boys. If you were trying to figure out your brother's predicted height, for example, you would add five inches to your mom's height and then add that number to your dad's height and divide by two.)

Taller than the Boys

Have you ever wondered why many sixth-grade girls are taller than the boys in their class? It's because lots of the girls have been in their growth spurts for a year or two, and most of the boys have a few years to go. Boys tend to start their growth spurts around age 11 or 12, and they usually grow fastest when they are about 13 or even older.

Ouch!

When you are growing so tall so fast, it might feel as if it hurts, which is where the term *growing pains* comes from. Especially if you play sports, a common spot for growing pains is on the upper shinbone just below the kneecap. To find this spot, sit in a chair and put three straight fingers below your kneecap. A growing pain is typically right where the third finger rests. This spot hurts because the tendon attaching the kneecap to the shinbone actually tugs on the bone, causing tenderness and sometimes even a visible bump. Doctors call this bump *Osgood Schlatter*.

You also might feel growing pains in your *calves*, or the backs of your lower legs. Here the muscles may feel pulled or cramped or may have a burning sensation. The pain can be felt anywhere along the lower leg, and sometimes even behind the knee.

For any growing pains, rubbing the area can help. So can ice or heat (get an adult's help when using heat). If you still hurt, talk to your doctor about whether or not to use pain medicine. After all, you don't want to miss out on sports and activities you enjoy just because you're growing!

If your pain involves more than just aches and cramps, such as joint swelling, a rash, a fever, or weakness, it's time to see the doctor.

Snooze Time

Going to bed early may seem like no fun, but getting your zzzs boosts your health and helps you grow.

Sleep isn't just something you do so that you're not tired in the morning. It also makes your whole body feel good.

Sleep for height. Did you know that you get taller when you head to bed? It's true! While you're sleeping, your brain releases extra *growth hormone*, which tells your bones to lengthen. (For more information about hormones, see page 28.) Your genes and the foods you eat play a big part, too. But if you want to give your body the best shot at growing well, sleep more!

Sleep for health. Sleep is important for keeping you healthy. It gives your body a break, allowing it to recover from the day. When you're sick and just want to crawl into bed and rest, sleep also helps you heal.

Sleep for relaxation. Without enough sleep, your body feels stressed, and it releases stress hormones. These hormones aren't good to have around all the time, and they can even slow down your growth. So get some sleep and give your body a break.

Sleep for happiness. If you've ever gone to bed too late and then had to get up early, you know how cranky you can be. Without enough sleep, it's easy to feel moody, overreact, or lose your cool over little things. Head to bed, and get happy!

How Many Zzzs Do I Need?

It may seem like a lot, but most growing bodies want at least 10 hours of sleep each night. That doesn't mean this will happen each and every night, but the closer you can get to this amount, the better.

But let's face it, after-school activities, sports, family dinners, and homework take up a lot of time. If you are waking up for school between 6:00 and 7:00 A.M., in order to get 10 hours of sleep you will need to go to bed between 8:00 and 9:00 P.M. each night. This can be tough! It's always best to get a good night's sleep every night, so when you can, get to bed early. But if your sleep routine falls short, then you do need to make up the missed hours—usually on the weekends. This is called "catch-up sleep": you can sleep in late, go to bed super early, or even take naps. Though catch-up sleep isn't as good as getting a consistent good night's sleep every night, it will help you feel more energized during the week.

If you're having problems drifting off to dreamland, don't be too hard on yourself. Some girls have trouble falling asleep at night, and then when they realize how late it is, they worry about not being asleep. This only makes things worse, because it can kick-start those stress hormones and wake you up even more! Instead of stressing out, distract yourself by taking some deep breaths, reading for a few minutes, or counting backward by threes from 100 to zero.

Maybe you have tried to get all the sleep you need by going to bed early, but you wake up at the crack of dawn and aren't tired anymore. That's OK! Your body is doing what it needs. Still aim for that early bedtime in case there are mornings when you are able to sleep a little bit later.

Tune Out

It's not great to watch TV, use a computer, or play video games right before bed, because these kinds of activities can turn your brain "on" and make you feel more awake. Some girls hear this advice and say, "No way! I zone out when I stare at a screen. It relaxes me." You may think it feels that way, but screen time actually causes your brain to be active instead of calm. So cut back on your screen time on weeknights as much as possible—do homework that requires a computer first, and save the paper-based projects for later in the evening.

Reading almost always relaxes the brain and helps you fall asleep. But don't pick a book that is too exciting or scary, because this can have the opposite effect! Reading a story that feels comfortable and soothing is a great way to wind down for sleep.

Keeping Clean

Soap is key in helping to keep you stink-free!

Suds Up

As you start to go through puberty, your body will make smells it never made before—and not great smells, either! Your feet may get stinky (a smell you may notice when you take your shoes and socks off after a long day at school). Or perhaps your feet will smell fine, but your armpits will not. Regardless of where the stink starts, washing with soap is a simple solution.

Whether you take a bath or a shower, use soap, lather it up, and wash yourself from head to toe. Use a washcloth, sponge, or loofah to help. Almost any soap will do, but if you have sensitive skin, stay away from soaps with dyes or perfumes, and skip using bubbles when taking a bath.

While most girls your age need to take a bath or shower every day, you don't need to wash your hair quite as often. Talk to your mom or dad about the best schedule for you.

Your *pubic area*, which is the V-shaped patch between your hip bones and your legs, also needs to be cleaned. But you may want to ditch the soap when you do because soap can be irritating. Just take a wet washcloth and gently wipe between the labia (see page 26) to clean the area.

Keep Your Hands Clean

When you touch something—such as a doorknob, a desk, or a computer keyboard—it is covered with germs from other people who have touched it before. Your body is meant to fight different kinds of germs naturally. But if you put your germ-covered fingers in your mouth (for example, when eating a sandwich or biting your nails), the germs can go right inside your body. And even though your body can fight off most germs most of the time, sometimes you may get sick.

Antibacterial hand sanitizers seem to be available just about everywhere you go: schools, grocery stores, doctors' offices. While hand sanitizers are OK to use when a sink isn't available, washing with soap and water (and making a good lather) is always the best choice.

The quick fix is to wash your hands, before you eat and *always* after you use the bathroom. That way all of the germs you've collected go right down the drain. Use soap and water and—if you can—wash for about 20 seconds, which is how long it takes to sing the "Happy Birthday" song twice.

Deodorants and Antiperspirants

Armpits can be particularly stinky areas because they get very hot and sweaty, and then that sweat combines with the bacteria that live on your skin to make you smell. You actually sweat (and can make smells) all over your body, but because the skin is folded over in the armpits, the sweat stays around longer, creating a better chance to stink. Other parts of the body where there isn't a lot of air breezing by—like sock-covered feet—sweat and smell the same way.

Lots of products are available to keep bad armpit smells away. Deodorants do what their name says: they de-odorize. This means that you'll still sweat but the sweat won't smell when deodorant is around. Antiperspirants are entirely different. These stop ("anti") sweating ("perspiration"). If you don't sweat in the first place, you won't smell. Some girls choose one type of product, some choose a combination (antiperspirant plus deodorant), and some choose none at all, sticking with bathing instead. A parent can help you decide what works best for you.

Pimple Prevention

If there are bumps and spots all over the place, it's not a human dot-to-dot game—it's probably just acne.

Zits Are the Pits

If you could look at your skin under a microscope, you'd see a bunch of tiny holes called *pores*. Pores release sweat to cool down the body. However, when you start puberty, *hormones* also tell your skin to make more oils. Those oils can clog pores, and bacteria that normally live on your skin can get trapped, too. Before you know it, pimples pop up. And since you have skin all over your body, that means you can get acne just about anywhere—most commonly on your face, neck, chest, scalp, and upper back.

Because the skin gets more oily during puberty, many girls think that using products (such as soaps, cleansers, and alcohol-based wipes) to dry out the skin will prevent pimples. But not necessarily! When you dry your skin, the oil glands beneath the surface sometimes get even more active, and they make more oils. So wash your skin with gentle soaps or cleansers, pat dry, and then apply a moisturizer to help slow down your oil-forming pores. Avoid products that contain overdrying alcohols such as *ethyl alcohol, ethanol,* and *isopropyl alcohol.*

If you do have pimples, **DON'T PICK.** Even if you think the bumps might look better a little bit flatter, popping a zit could create new problems. The picked area becomes even more irritated and can get infected—this can mean an obvious scab or, even worse, a permanent scar.

Hands Off

When it comes to keeping acne away, it's all about what you put on your skin—and that includes your hands! Some people think acne is related to what you eat, but that's true only if you touch your face with hands that have touched food. So eating a greasy pizza won't create a pimple, but if you wipe your greasy hands on your face, a zit could follow.

Go Away

There are lots of different ways to help make acne less troublesome.

- Wash your face every morning and every night, and don't forget to moisturize.

- Remove dirt using a gentle cleanser or soap that is free of dyes and perfumes.

- Don't scrub too hard, or you can irritate your skin.

- Avoid oily facial products and cosmetics that can make acne worse. If you really want to ditch the zits, try water-based products instead.

- Some girls use special cleansers, creams, or even medicines to help control their acne. This should be done only with the help of a doctor. Here are some of the treatments you may hear about and how they work:
  - *Antibiotic:* kills the bacteria growing in clogged pores.
  - *Benzoyl peroxide:* works as an antibiotic and also helps to unclog pores.
  - *Retinoid:* prevents pore clogging.

Are the bumps on my upper arms acne, too?

Nope! Many girls will have tiny skin-colored bumps on the backs of their upper arms at some point during puberty. These are super small—about the size of a pencil tip—and feel a little rough. But they don't itch, and they won't get bigger or redder. They are called *keratosis pillaris,* a fancy way of saying bumpy skin. The bumps might disappear a bit if you keep your skin soft, so try using a washcloth or loofah in the shower and apply moisturizer regularly. But truly it is time that helps them go away.

Help! Q&A

Girls just like you sent us their body questions. Here are the answers!

I'm really skinny for a 10-year-old. My friends make rude comments and say I look like a stick. I told them that my doctor said I'm fine, but they think I'm lying.
Not Too Thin

It can sting when friends make comments about the way you look. Next time it happens, say, "Please don't call me that. It makes me feel awful." It could be that your friends are just being insensitive, and telling them that they're hurting you could fix this. But it also could be that they are worried about you. Some girls are naturally very thin, but other girls sometimes do dangerous things to try to make themselves thin. It can be tough for a friend to tell the difference. Talk it through. If they're not convinced, ask your mom to assure them that you really are OK.

I sweat a lot. I use deodorant, but it doesn't seem to help. I'm starting to get uncomfortable at school, and I don't have time between classes to wash up. What should I do?
It's the Pits

Sweat is totally natural—your body makes it so that your skin can cool down more quickly. The problem is, sweat can show on your clothes, and after a while it can make you smell. Here are some things you can try: Take a bath or a shower every day and make sure to lather well with soap. Consider using an anti-perspirant that will keep the sweating to a minimum or using a different brand than the deodorant you're using now. If you're seeing sweat on your clothes, try wearing looser-fitting tops. A loose shirt will keep you cooler because it allows air to swirl around your body, and it won't show sweat nearly as much as a fitted shirt can. If none of this works, talk to your doctor.

I think I'm overweight. I've tried going on diets, but I just can't stay on them. I'm scared that my friends will make fun of me when I wear a tank top or a swimsuit. What should I do?
Too Big

The first step is to check in with someone who can tell you if you actually are overweight. It can be very hard to tell when a growing body needs to lose weight, so talk to your parents and ask to go to the doctor to get weighed and measured. Whether or not you're overweight, your body needs enough of the right fuel in order to work and grow properly. You can hurt yourself if you're not getting proper nutrition, so dieting isn't something for any girl to tackle alone. If your parents and your doctor say that you do need to lose weight, then you can come up with a healthy plan together.

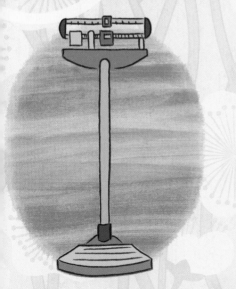

I'm tired all the time! I get a full night's sleep, but when my alarm clock goes off in the morning for school, I feel as if I could sleep for another day. My best friend is constantly full of energy, but I always feel like a zombie. What's wrong with me?
Too Tired

There's probably nothing to worry about. After all, your body needs lots of rest to deal with growing. And as you get older, your natural wake-up time might get later, which can make you want to go back to sleep after your alarm goes off. This is totally normal. It's great that you're getting a good night's sleep every night, but you might try going to bed earlier, if you can. (Think of it as a trick for getting more sleep, not as having an early bedtime.) And some extra sleep on the weekends might make you feel better, too, so sleep in or even take a nap every once in a while. If you feel really tired—so tired that you can hardly get out of bed or you feel as if you could fall asleep in school—then it's time to see your doctor. Some medical conditions can make you feel sluggish, so a doctor can check to make sure that you're healthy.

Girl Stuff

Your body parts are all the same as when you were a baby, but now they're getting bigger! If you learn about the power of hormones, you'll understand why your breasts grow, new hair appears, and eventually all girls get their period. It's a lot of change going on in one body, but it happens slowly and at a pace that's right for you.

The Anatomy of You

Take a closer peek at your body parts.

Body Language

As your body starts to change and different parts develop, you may have questions about how or why things *look* different. You might experience aches, pains, or just new sensations, making you wonder why your body *feels* different.

Just as you are changing on the outside, you are also changing inside. You've had the same organs your whole life, but you may never have given them much thought. Every organ has a unique job. You know that the heart pumps your blood and the lungs breathe in oxygen. Well, other parts, like the urinary tract, help remove waste from your body. And the organs in the reproductive tract will be responsible for helping you to have a baby when you are an adult. Even though you cannot see most of these parts, it is just as important to be familiar with what is inside as with what is outside.

Talking about your body isn't always easy, but knowing what each part does and how to call it by the correct name can make it a little less challenging. Sometimes it is embarrassing to use such formal-sounding words, but they are appropriate, and using them can help adults better understand and respond to your concerns.

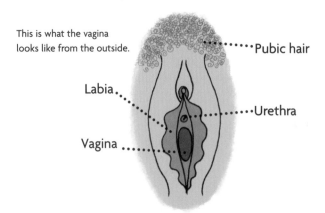

This is what the vagina looks like from the outside.

Pubic hair

Labia

Urethra

Vagina

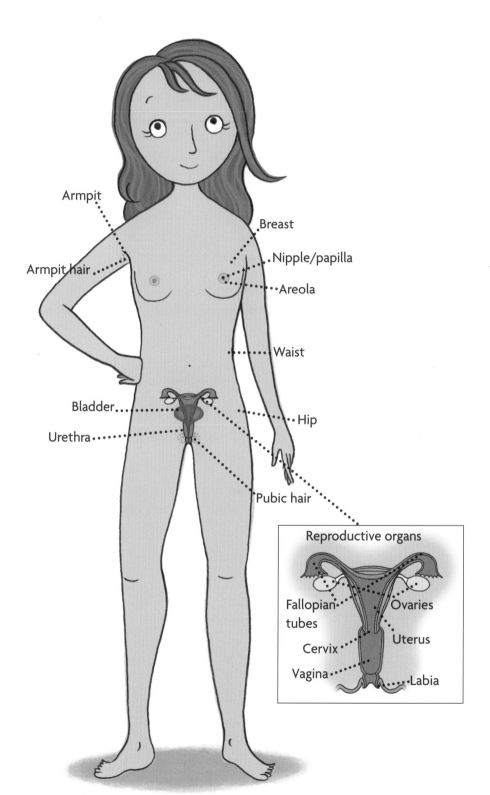

Armpit

Armpit hair

Breast

Nipple/papilla

Areola

Waist

Bladder

Urethra

Hip

Pubic hair

Reproductive organs

Fallopian tubes

Ovaries

Cervix

Uterus

Vagina

Labia

Hormones

When it's time for puberty to start, it's hormones that tell your body "go!"

All Kinds of Hormones

Your body actually makes lots of different hormones, not just the ones involved in having a period. Here are some other hormones you might hear about:

Thyroid hormone: The way your body burns energy is called *metabolism.* Thyroid hormone affects your body's metabolism throughout the day and night.

Insulin: This hormone helps sugar get inside cells so that it can be used for energy. People with diabetes either don't have enough insulin or the insulin they have doesn't work the way it should. This is why their blood sugar level is high—the sugar has a hard time getting inside the cells and instead stays in the bloodstream.

Growth hormone: This does just what its name says— it helps you grow! Growth hormone also affects almost every organ in your body, so it will still be important when you are an adult.

How Do Hormones Work?

Since puberty starts at different times for different people, how does your body know when to begin? *Hormones.* You produce these natural chemicals that travel all around your body, sending important messages, telling organs what to do or how to grow. For puberty, four main hormones control what's going on:

estrogen: causes breast development and helps to regulate your menstrual cycle once you start getting your period.

progesterone: similar to estrogen, this hormone also helps to regulate your menstrual cycle once you start getting your period.

FSH (short for follicule-stimulating hormone): tells an egg in one of your ovaries to mature.

LH (short for luteinizing hormone): tells an egg in one of your ovaries to release itself, also known as *ovulation.*

Once puberty starts, different parts of your body "talk" through these hormones. Your brain sends a hormone message to your ovaries, and in response, your ovaries send hormone messages back to your brain. Though you've had some of these hormones in your body since you were a baby, once you enter puberty, there are many more of them! All this actually starts well before your period ever begins, but when you do get your period for the first time, there's still a lot of adjusting going on inside to help estrogen, progesterone, FSH, and LH learn to rise and fall at the right times. Sometimes these hormones shift in a perfect pattern from the very start, but sometimes it can take months for all of these hormones to get into a regular rhythm.

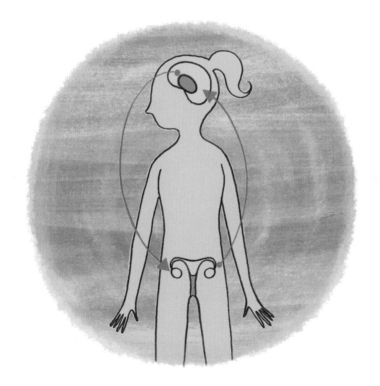

Flat Chest to New Breasts

As you enter puberty, developing breasts are sometimes the first changes to appear.

Know as You Grow

As you read in *The Care and Keeping of You,* breast development is divided into five stages. First, you start with a flat chest, and next you move on to breast buds. Breast buds can be tender—they can hurt when you bump into something or feel funny just wearing a tight shirt. This is all normal. Long after the breast buds first appear (sometimes many months and sometimes even years later), your breasts continue to grow. One side might grow bigger than the other, but they should even out eventually.

Breasts take a long time to grow. It can be four or five years from the time you notice your first breast bud until your "adult" breasts are fully grown. In fact, it takes so long that some girls wonder, "Will it ever stop?" Yes! Breasts definitely stop growing, but they also change throughout your life.

Many girls notice that around the time of their period, their breasts get a little bit bigger and more tender. This *swelling* happens because the hormones in your body that are responsible for your period also affect the way your breasts look and feel from day to day. So when you have more of certain hormones during the week of your period, you also may have more swelling in your breasts.

Nipple Knowledge

Just as your breasts grow and change, so do your nipples. There are two parts to the nipple: the big round base is called the *areola,* and the smaller, taller part is called the *papilla* (although most people simply call this part the nipple). When you develop breast buds, the areola grows slightly bigger and the papilla sticks up a little. Over the years that your breasts grow, the areola usually gets darker and the papilla sticks out even more.

Nipples can look different from girl to girl. Sometimes girls have small bumps on their areolas about the size of half of a grain of rice. These bumps are completely normal. Other girls will notice a few hairs on the skin around the areola. This is also normal. And some girls will have really dark nipples while others will have very light ones. Guess what? This is normal, too.

Lumps and Bumps

Since a breast begins as a small bump under the nipple, you can see that lumps and bumps in breasts are normal. However, you may also have heard that breast cancer can be felt as a lump. So how do you know if your breasts are healthy? First of all, it's **really, really** rare for girls and teenagers to get breast cancer. And second, breast tissue is not perfectly smooth and soft—lumps and bumps are normal in breasts. At your checkups, your doctor will examine your breasts to make sure they are healthy.

Outside of your doctor visits, you can do your own monthly breast self-exams. This is something that older women do about once a month to check their breasts for lumps and bumps that shouldn't be there. While it's not something you have to do, you can start checking yourself when you are young. That way you can get in the habit before becoming an adult and learn where your own normal lumps and bumps are.

Self-Exam How-To

There are many different techniques for breast self-exams. This one is very easy. Either lie down on your bed or stand up straight somewhere that is private, such as in the shower. Raise one arm above your head as if you are raising your hand in class. This is the side you are going to examine. With your other hand, hold your index and middle fingers out straight, keeping your thumb, ring finger, and pinky tucked in. You're ready to begin.

Imagine that your breast is a clock. You are going to start at the top, or 12 o'clock.

Rest your two extended fingers on your upper chest before the mound of your breast begins, and make small circles with your fingers pressing against your skin.

Now lift your fingers off and move them a little closer to the nipple, but still at 12 o'clock. Make the small circles again. It will take three or four moves toward the nipple before you are done with 12 o'clock.

Once you are done, move to one o'clock and start over, out far enough that you aren't touching the mound of the breast at first.

Once you have gone all the way around, switch so that the other arm is raised above your head and examine that breast. It usually takes a couple of minutes on each side to get all the way around. Don't press so hard that you hurt yourself, and remember that at your age lumps, bumps, and tenderness are all normal.

After examining each breast, you can squeeze the nipple very gently. You just want to make sure no green or yellow liquid comes out. This is called *discharge*. If it comes out of the nipple, a doctor should check it out.

Remember, most of the tender lumps and bumps you have are normal, but if you are still worried, you can always ask your doctor or your mom to help with your exam.

Best Bras for You

Find the support you need.

Beyond Your First Bra

Once you have started wearing bras, such as the ones covered in *The Care and Keeping of You*, things will continue to change. As you grow, your first bra will become too small both in the cup and in the rib size, and it will no longer provide the support you need.

When you find a bra that feels comfortable, buy one or two but don't spend a fortune on a dozen, because your body may change again very soon. As your breasts swell during your period, a bra that fits perfectly during another part of the month could feel too tight. To help, have different bras that fit during different times.

Form Fitting

As your breasts get bigger, pay attention to what type of bra fits best. Here's a good general rule: you get support from the bottom of your bra more than from the top of your bra. Although bra straps are very helpful, it's especially important to choose a bra with a strong elastic band across your chest or a wire underneath the cups. If you don't have any support from the bottom, you might notice that the straps dig into your shoulders, creating crease lines in your skin or even making your shoulders uncomfortable.

If you develop bigger breasts, they might feel very heavy. You probably won't feel this way all the time, but running, climbing stairs, and other activities with a lot of movement might become uncomfortable. Girls with larger breasts sometimes complain of back or neck pain, which is why the fit of your bra is important. Good fit means you won't feel the weight of your breasts in the same way, so you are less likely to have aches and pains. Also, well-supported breasts don't move as much, making up-and-down motions no big deal.

When Both Sides Aren't the Same

Since it's normal for your breasts to grow at different rates, with one getting bigger before the other, bra designers have come to the rescue! Most bras have adjustable shoulder straps so that you can make one side a little shorter or longer than the other. Some bras come with padding tucked into the material of the bra. You can remove the padding on your bigger side but keep it in on the smaller side so that the bra feels more comfortable and your breasts look more even.

Styles

There are tons of bra choices out there! The type of bra you'll choose will depend upon what fits the best and also what clothing you are wearing. Here's a quick guide for the most common styles you'll find:

standard: one strap over each shoulder, and the fastener is in the back.

front close: one strap over each shoulder, but the fastener is between the cups in the front, not in the back.

crisscross or racer-back: one strap over each shoulder, but the straps either cross in the back making an "X" or they merge in the back making a "Y"—these styles often work well with tank tops.

strapless: no straps at all. Instead, these bras have extra support around the middle so that they can stay up on their own. You usually wear this kind of bra with a special dress or top.

sports: one strap over each shoulder, but extra material throughout so that the bra looks more like the top half of a one-piece sports bathing suit than the top half of a bikini.

Bras can look super cute at the store, especially if they have bright colors or unique patterns. But your body is private, and you don't really want other people to see what you are wearing under your clothes. A colored bra underneath a black T-shirt won't be noticeable, but it will be very obvious when you wear light-colored tops. Think about choosing bras in colors close to your own skin tone so that they don't show through your clothes.

A Hairy Situation

Here's what you need to know when unexpected body hair begins to sprout up.

More Hair . . . Everywhere

As you go through puberty, you will likely get more hair in some places and new hair in others. The hair you have on your legs and maybe even on your arms will probably get a little darker or thicker. All eyes are most likely NOT on you, but when you feel as if they are, talk to your parents to get honest advice about how your body hair looks.

New hair will come in under your arms. And you'll also begin to see hair in your pubic area. This hair is called *pubic hair*. At first, these hairs might be fine and straight— some girls have some from the time they are babies. But as you go through puberty, the hairs will become thick, dark, and curly.

Pubic hair grows in your pubic area on the *labia,* the folds of skin between your legs leading to the vagina. At the beginning of puberty, this hair stays just around the labia. After a while, you will notice that the hair covers a larger triangle, appearing closer to your underwear lines. By the time you are almost an adult, it is normal to notice a few pubic hairs on your upper thighs.

Some girls get hair under their arms before they get it on the labia; others do the opposite. Sometimes hair appears way before your breasts begin to grow and sometimes long after. There isn't a right order here—everyone's body is unique.

Safe Shaving

When girls start growing more hair, often they want to remove it, especially from their legs and armpits. Shaving with a razor is a common hair-removal option. But just because your friend is shaving doesn't mean you have to do the same. While you may notice your increased body hair, almost no one else will! However, if you think you're ready to start shaving, talk it over with a parent first.

Follicle Facts

Hair grows out of tiny pores in the skin called *follicles*. Most of the time, when you remove hair, the hair will grow back. And when it does, the new hair can become *ingrown*, curling inside the follicle and having trouble finding the right way out.

An ingrown hair can cause irritation, forming a little bump that might be red. Doctors call any inflammation of the follicle *folliculitis*. Sometimes bacteria will get trapped, causing a small infection. Because each little follicle can become inflamed, you might notice one reddish spot or you might see dozens.

If you have folliculitis, show a parent. You may need to have your skin checked by a doctor, and sometimes you will need to take an antibiotic if the area is infected. To prevent folliculitis, follow these tips:

- Always use a clean (never old or rusty!) razor.
- To avoid ingrown hairs, try a gentle loofah or washcloth when you lather with soap. This helps hairs find their way to the skin surface.
- Always use your own razor, washcloth, and loofah.
- Never pick at your skin—it can easily become infected.

Skipping the Razor

Shaving is not the only way to remove hair. There are many other choices, but each has pros and cons. Hair removal is a very personal decision. However, many of the following non-shaving choices come with their share of risks, so it's up to your parents to decide what's right for you.

Tweezing: This means plucking out the hair with a pair of tweezers. Tweezing can hurt because you pull out the entire hair and its root. It also takes a long time. Since you pluck hairs one at a time, it would take a REALLY long time to tweeze an entire leg! But tweezing can be used for random hairs scattered here and there that bother you.

Depilatory: This is a fancy name for a chemical that makes your hair fall out. In general, a depilatory comes as a cream that you smear onto the surface where the hair will be removed. After several minutes, the depilatory is washed off and the hair washes off with it. While this doesn't hurt like tweezing and it's a lot faster, depilatories can cause skin irritation. Also, most of these creams smell really bad. So if you have sensitive skin (or a sensitive nose!), this is not a good option for you.

Waxing: A professional applies warm wax onto the skin where the hair is going to be removed. A cloth is placed over the wax, patted until it sticks to the wax, and then pulled quickly off the skin. The wax comes off with the cloth, pulling the hair along with it. Waxing can be uncomfortable and even painful because the hairs are pulled out quickly. When a professional removes the hair this way, she needs to be careful that the wax is not too hot—if it is, your skin can get burned.

Bleaching: Although it doesn't remove hair, bleaching lightens hair. Bleaching the hair turns it from dark to light, so that the hair seems to disappear if your skin is fair. The downside of bleaching is that sensitive skin might become red or itchy from the chemicals in the bleach.

If you decide that shaving is right for you, keep these tips in mind.

• Skin is softest when it's wet, so shaving in the shower or bath or over the sink reduces the likelihood of cutting your skin. Never shave dry unless you are using an electric razor. (And when using an electric razor, be sure to follow the manufacturer's instructions carefully.)

• Slick up your skin with shaving cream or soap.

• Use short, careful strokes. Don't apply a lot of pressure.

• Rinse the razor frequently so that it doesn't get clogged with hair.

• Replace your razor blade after two or three uses. A sharp blade is the secret to a smooth shave. Dull blades cause nicks, and rusty blades can carry infection.

Period Basics

Let's get right to the point.

The Facts
Since the most basic facts about periods are covered in *The Care and Keeping of You,* you probably already know that a period, short for *menstrual period,* is the time each month when a woman loses some blood through her vagina.

This bleeding is totally normal. Once you start getting your period, approximately every month your uterus builds a thin lining—called the *uterine lining*—out of blood and tissue. This lining is preparing the uterus for a baby one day. But for now, it's just part of a regular rhythm in your body. At the end of that month, the lining is shed. And the only way out is through your vagina.

When you bleed from your period, you will notice that the blood can look thick or thin, stringy or clumpy, bright red or dark brownish. These are all normal. Also if you look closely, you will notice that your *urine* (pee) is not red—it's still yellow. That's because the blood comes from your vagina, but the urine comes from the urethra, which is right next door (see page 27).

Why Every Month?
The lining in the uterus needs to stay healthy. It grows for a few weeks, but after that it needs to be released and replaced with a newer, healthier lining. This schedule is controlled by your hormones—the very same hormones that make your acne pop out and your breasts grow.

When Is It Going to Start?
Some girls get their period for the first time when they are in elementary school, while others don't get it until high school. This is all normal. It's almost impossible to predict when you will start getting your period. Generally, girls have been in puberty for a while by the time it happens—they usually have breasts and pubic hair, too. But each body is different, and there is no exact time line for how each person develops.

Probably the best way of guessing at what age you will get your period for the first time is to ask your mom when she got hers. Many girls (but certainly not all) get their period at about the same age that their moms did. By asking your mom, you can also start a conversation about how your body is changing, and if you are nervous, your mom can help to reassure you.

Period Pains

Periods can come with new sensations in your body.

Aches and Pains

One of the most common fears about getting your period for the first time is being uncertain about what it will feel like. And like everything about periods, it's different for every girl. Some girls might have aches and pains, while others feel no different than they do every other day.

The bleeding from your period doesn't feel like any other kind of bleeding—there's no stinging or burning because nothing is being "cut." However, you may feel *cramps*. Cramps are achy pains that can go along with the shedding of the uterine lining. Most girls are not bothered by cramps. Either they don't notice them in the first place, or they notice them but they can still go on with their usual activities.

Sometimes, though, cramps hurt. They often get better when you wear loose clothing around your waist. If a cramp feels especially bad, sit down or even lie down to help the cramp go away. If you are able and have help from an adult, you might try putting a heating pad on your lower belly. There are also medicines that can make cramp pains less severe, but you shouldn't take these without talking to a parent first.

The best news here is that cramps get better. They feel less painful as your period gets lighter, and they usually go away as you get older. In fact, most girls who experience cramp pains when they are young outgrow them entirely. The goal is to keep your routine as regular as possible when you are having your period. Eating a healthy diet and getting exercise will make your cramps feel better, so keep up your good habits!

Pinches and Pangs

Another new sensation you might feel is a tiny little pang—a sharp pinch—on one side or the other of your belly a couple of weeks before your period. This is the pinch of *middleschmirtz*, when an egg is getting ready to be released from one of your ovaries. Remember that your ovaries are located close to your hips, and that one egg is released from one ovary each month about two weeks before your period. One day, one of those eggs might become a baby, but for now, your body is just practicing and getting into a routine. Most of the time you won't feel a thing, but some girls do. The feeling is like being pinched on the inside, but it doesn't last long.

That Time of the Month

You probably won't be able to set your clock to your period, but it doesn't have to be a complete surprise either.

Period Predictability

You won't always know when your period will arrive, because periods have their own schedules. But there are some ways to predict when your period is coming, how long it's staying, and when it's going. The timing of your menstrual cycle is not an exact science and is based more on "**usuallys**":

• A period **usually** lasts about a week, but it can be shorter or longer and still be normal.

• The heaviest bleeding is **usually** in the first couple of days.

• Periods **usually** happen about every four weeks, counting from the first day of one period to the first day of the next period.

Period UN-Predictability

A period that happens in a pattern every few weeks is called a *regular period*. (It's usually about every four weeks, but for some girls "regular" means having periods come every three weeks or every five weeks.) The benefit of having a regular period is that you can guess when your period is most likely going to come. But don't be surprised if it isn't regular.

In the beginning, it's common to get a period and then not get another for many weeks or even months. Sometimes your period timing will be all over the place—your periods might happen two weeks apart, then seven weeks apart, then three weeks apart. While this can be very annoying, it is normal.

Keep Track

The easiest way to tell whether your period is regular is to keep a calendar. Most girls don't want to write the word "period" on the calendar because it's private, and they don't necessarily want everyone—particularly a brother or sister—to know what's going on with them. Instead you can put a symbol or initials on the date that your period starts, and if you want to, you can also make a note of when it ends. If you keep track this way, you will begin to learn your body's pattern.

Overflow

There is such a thing as having your period too often. Remember that when you get your period, you lose a little bit of blood—only about two to three tablespoons total—and your body needs to replace that blood by making more. If you get your period repeatedly every couple of weeks or if your period lasts several days and the flow is quite heavy, your body might not be able to make new blood as quickly as it needs to. This can lead to having a low red-blood-cell count, which is called *anemia*.

If you develop anemia, you may feel very tired and draggy or even light-headed. Your skin can look pale because there aren't as many red blood cells floating around your body. It is very easy for a doctor to test for anemia, so if you are concerned about it, let one of your parents know.

To avoid anemia in the first place or to make it go away, eat foods rich in iron, such as beans (black, pinto, soy, and lentils), dark green leafy veggies (spinach, kale, brussels sprouts, and broccoli), lean red meats (beef and lamb), and seafood (especially sardines and shrimp). Many cereals and grains also have iron added to them, so look for "iron-fortified" on the label.

Tampon Tips

While pads are always a perfect first choice, here are some tips when you want to try tampons.

How to Insert a Tampon

For most girls, using a tampon is a little scary at first because it involves a part of the body that may be unfamiliar. If you are too nervous to touch or look at (or even think about!) your vagina, you aren't ready to use a tampon.

For girls who are ready, there's nothing to worry about. With patience and practice, you'll be a pro in no time. Be sure to carefully read the instructions that come in the box of tampons, and talk to your mom or a trusted female adult. The steps are pretty simple:

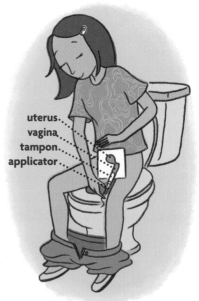

uterus
vagina
tampon
applicator

1. Get Ready

Wash your hands. Remove the outer wrapper of the tampon. Hold the applicator tube with your thumb, middle finger, and index finger as shown. With the other hand, find the labia outside the opening of the vagina. Use your fingers to spread apart the labia, which opens the vagina.

2. Insert

Insert the tip of the applicator, aiming at a slight upward angle toward your back. Relax your muscles. Guide the first half of the applicator into your vagina. Then push on the inner tube of the applicator with your index finger. This will push the tampon all the way out through the applicator and into your vagina. Pull out the applicator and throw it away.

3. Check Fit

The string should now hang down between your thighs. If the tampon is in correctly, you won't be able to feel it. If it feels uncomfortable, it may be in crooked or may not be in far enough. You can use your finger to gently push it up farther, or you can pull it out and start over with a new tampon. Wash your hands afterward.

4. Removal

When it's time to take out the tampon, sit down on the toilet, relax your muscles, and pull down on the string. The tampon will slide out of your vagina. It's not a good idea to flush the tampon down the toilet—this can clog drains. Instead, wrap the tampon in toilet paper and throw it out. Wash your hands when you're done.

Tampons Versus Pads

Most girls use pads when they first get their period. But once a girl's period becomes regular and she's gotten more comfortable with her changing body (particularly her vagina), she may want to use tampons. Here are some things to think about if you're considering making the switch:

- There's no rush. Pads stay outside of your body, and that works better for some girls. Tampons are not something you ever have to try.

- Practice makes perfect. Before you ever insert a tampon into your body, you will want to see how it works. Open a tampon wrapper and check out the applicator, figuring out how the actual tampon gets released. Some girls put the tampon in a small cup of water to see how much liquid it can absorb.

- The string won't break! When you look closely at a tampon, you will see that the string is part of the same material that makes the tampon. This adds strength so that the string cannot break off. The tampon will not get stuck inside your body!

- Once you start using tampons, you will probably also still use pads. Tampons are convenient during the day, but most girls use pads for overnight.

- Some girls choose to switch to tampons because of sports—with a lot of activity, they find that tampons are a little more comfortable.

- Many girls choose to try tampons when it's time to swim, since pads aren't designed for water. But if you're not ready to use tampons, that's fine! If you are having your period on a hot summer day, just wear a pair of shorts and find other fun things to do outside instead of swimming.

- Tampons require keeping track of time. It is not safe to keep a tampon in your body for long periods of time. You should change a tampon at least every four to six hours. This means that if you put in a tampon before the school day starts, you will have to change it at least once at school.

Infections

Keep your body clean and practice good hygiene to prevent a pubic area infection.

Good Hygiene

You've heard how important it is to use good hygiene. For instance, you know you should wash your hands regularly—before eating, after using the bathroom, after touching something dirty—to help keep you from getting sick and spreading germs to other people. The same good hygiene applies to the rest of your body. Keeping your pubic area clean and changing pads or tampons often can help you avoid getting irritation or even infections.

Infection Information

The three most-talked-about female infections have different causes and symptoms:

Urinary tract infection (UTI): Your *urinary tract* is the part of your body that makes urine and helps it get out of your body. Urine is made by your kidneys, it's stored in your bladder, and then it comes down a little tube and out an opening next to your vagina called the urethra. A UTI is caused by bacteria that grow somewhere along that path. Why do bacteria grow there? They usually grow when people hold their urine for a long time. When you have a UTI, it will probably sting when you pee. Some girls have stomach aches or nausea; others feel as if they have to go to the bathroom constantly, but when they try, very little (or nothing) comes out. Occasionally a UTI will cause fever. If you think you have a UTI, let one of your parents know. Your parent can take you to the doctor, where you can have a simple test to check—usually all you need to do is pee into a special cup.

Yeast infection: Yeast infections aren't typically painful, but if you have one, you'll notice white discharge that can look thick, almost like cottage cheese. And sometimes your vagina will itch. A yeast infection is caused by a fungus that likes to grow in dark, hot, sweaty places. Your vagina is dark and easily becomes hot and sweaty when you are exercising or even just sitting around on a hot day. The best way to prevent a yeast infection is to air yourself out—this means wearing loose-fitting cotton bottoms when it is hot, and getting out of tight underpants and wearing very loose bottoms or just a nightgown overnight. If you think you have a yeast infection, talk to one of your parents and see a doctor. And if you do have a yeast infection, avoid doing things that make you hotter and sweatier down there—such as bike riding or sitting in a wet bathing suit—until the infection is gone.

Toxic shock syndrome: Toxic shock is the rarest of the infections, but it's the scariest, too. One way it is caused is by bacteria that can grow if you leave a tampon inside of you for too long. When a person gets toxic shock, she becomes very ill—symptoms include high fever, vomiting, diarrhea, spreading rash, weakness, and confusion. Toxic shock is so unusual that you will probably never know anyone who has had it. But it is so serious that all females are told to change their tampons every few hours.

Body Talk

Your changing body will probably lead to a lot of questions. Finding a trusted adult can help!

To Share or Not to Share?

The whole topic of your changing body and periods can feel embarrassing. Sometimes it feels as if everyone around you must know what's going on with your body. But think about it: when you walk down the street, close to one quarter of all teenage girls and women who pass you will be having their period. You've probably never thought about it like that before. And since you have never really known when someone else has her period, it's likely that no one else will automatically know about yours.

Periods can be a topic you want to keep private. That's fine! There are lots of things about your body that you want to keep to yourself. Remember, though, it is always best to have an adult you can talk to—someone who can help you when you are worried that something is not normal.

Mom's been there before. It may feel difficult to find alone time when you can talk about these things, but make up an excuse—tell your mom you want to go for a walk or join her when she's running an errand. Your mom is a great resource because she loves you, she has been where you are now, and her job is to keep you safe and healthy.

Don't forget about your dad! Just because he isn't a girl doesn't mean that your dad won't understand. It's great to talk to a parent, someone who is available to you 24 hours a day.

Pick an adult you can trust. Other trusted adults include your doctor, your teacher or school counselor, your coach, or other relatives such as an aunt or a grandparent. While your friends may really want to help you, it's not always smart to go to someone your own age for help with body questions. Even if they say they do, they probably don't know more than you do!

A Doctor's Help

Always talk to your parents first. But there will be times when you (and your parents) really need a doctor's advice. For example:

- You have been having heavy bleeding for several days, and your period just doesn't seem to be letting up. Now you feel a little dizzy or nauseated.
- You are having really bad stomach pains that make it difficult for you to participate in your regular activities or that take away your appetite.
- Your vaginal discharge seems to be a different color or have a much stronger smell than usual.

Body Boundaries

Your body is **your** body. That means that the only person who has the right to touch it or even look closely at it is you. The two exceptions to this rule are related to your health: your parents can check your body and so can a doctor (when a parent is in the room). But that's it. No one else can tell you that it is all right for them to touch or look closely at you unless it's OK with you. Understanding these boundaries keeps you safe. Talk to a trusted adult if someone tells you otherwise.

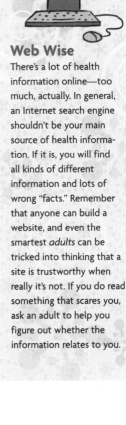

Web Wise

There's a lot of health information online—too much, actually. In general, an Internet search engine shouldn't be your main source of health information. If it is, you will find all kinds of different information and lots of wrong "facts." Remember that anyone can build a website, and even the smartest *adults* can be tricked into thinking that a site is trustworthy when really it's not. If you do read something that scares you, ask an adult to help you figure out whether the information relates to you.

Help! Q&A

Girls just like you sent us their puberty-related body questions. Here are the answers!

When I'm wearing a bathing suit, my pubic hair sticks out a little. I think it's super embarrassing. Can I shave it? If not, what should I do?
Hairy

Here's some good news—you have a lot of options here. A swimsuit with a boy-short shape could completely cover your hair without you having to do anything. You also could try adding some cute board shorts to your swim outfit. But if you decide that you need to do something about the hair, you have more choices, including shaving, waxing, or using a depilatory cream that removes hair. You might feel embarrassed to bring it up, but you must talk to a parent before you decide to remove the hair.

All of my friends are developed except for me. I feel left out. What should I do?
Wait for Me

Ugh. Why can't puberty happen exactly when you want it to? The first girls to start growing can feel awkward, and the last girls to develop often feel left behind. Unfortunately, there's nothing you can do to make your breasts grow, no matter what you might hear. That will happen only when it's the right time for your body. For now, focus on the things you can control—how well you eat, how much you exercise, and how much you sleep. Developing good habits will help keep you healthy all the way through puberty. And hang in there—it might seem as if it'll never happen, but it will.

I really want to shave my legs, but my mom says I'm not responsible enough. I'm so self-conscious about it. I do all I can to help around the house. How can I prove to her that I'm responsible enough?
Ready to Shave

Shaving is a different kind of responsibility than, say, remembering to clean your room. Your mom probably is worried about shaving because if you mess up even a little, you can really hurt yourself. A razor blade is super sharp. It can cut your skin easily, and shaving nicks can sting like crazy. So talk to your mom about how you feel about your legs and ask if you can compromise. If she's not comfortable with you starting to shave, she might be OK with another form of hair removal.

I haven't started my period yet, but I do have this white, creamy-looking stuff in my panties. Is it OK to put a tampon in for that?
Confused

No need for tampons yet. They're meant to soak up blood and are not designed to deal with the discharge you're describing—that's the whitish stuff in your underwear. The vagina makes discharge to keep itself clean, and many girls have a little bit of discharge in their underwear every day (usually about the size of a nickel). For some girls it looks clear, for others a little more off-white, and it's nothing to worry about. If you want to, you can put a very thin pad called a panty liner into your underwear. It'll catch the discharge but is so thin that you won't feel it. Otherwise, discharge simply gets washed off your underwear in the laundry.

My mom thinks it's time for me to wear a bra, but every time she buys me one, it's so uncomfortable. What can I do to find the right bra?
Bad Bras

First, ask yourself if the bras you have are actually uncomfortable or if you're just uncomfortable about wearing a bra. It's true that bras can sometimes make you feel self-conscious, and it's hard to feel good in a bra until you feel good about bras. The thing is, when you buy the right one and get used to it, bras can feel just fine. But you have to try on lots of them—sometimes it feels like a gazillion!—to find the right one. Instead of having her bring bras home to you, go shopping with your mom. Try on different sizes to find your fit, and then try on as many different styles as you can find. It might be frustrating to go through so many that don't feel good, but it'll be worth it when you finally find a bra you like.

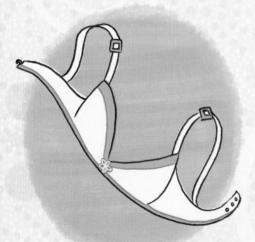

One of my breasts is developing and the other one isn't. When I look at them in a mirror, it feels as if the other one will never grow. Will I end up with only one breast? Please help!
Lopsided

Breasts often grow at different rates on the same person. So do legs and arms and fingernails. But with breasts, the difference can seem a little more noticeable. The first thing to remember is that this is normal. The second is that your two breasts should eventually even out. And the third thing—and this is really true—is that you probably notice this much more than anyone else does. Sometimes the things about our bodies that bother us the most seem so obvious, but really no one else pays any attention to them. If your breasts stay unequal, though, talk to a parent or your doctor.

I'm really scared of using tampons. My mom says it's fine to use pads for the rest of my life. But will people think I'm weird?
Scared of Tampons

It's no one else's business whether you use pads or tampons. After all, you don't really know what other women around you are using, so there's no reason for anyone to know about your choice, either. And your mom is right: there are some women who always choose pads over tampons. That is absolutely OK. You might change your mind as you get older, but for now, stick with whatever makes you comfortable. If your friends give you a hard time for using pads, you can say, "That's what works for me—what's the big deal?"

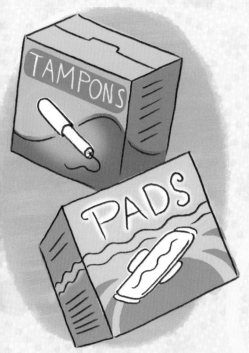

In school we have to go swimming for gym and take showers. I have my period and really don't want to wear a tampon, but what do I do when I have to be in the water?
Worried About Leaks

Every teacher and coach at school knows that girls your age can have their periods. So if you're scheduled to swim but you aren't ready for tampons—which is fine—then all you need to do is explain the situation. Talk to your teacher privately before school or before class and ask for an alternative to swimming. It's easier if you make it fast and direct: "I have my period today. I don't use tampons, so I need to do something other than swim." If you're too embarrassed to say it, try writing a note. You also can ask a parent to let your teacher know what's up. As for showering at school, use the bathroom right before, wipe really well, and then take a lightning-fast rinse in the shower. If you're still worried about showering, talk to your parent or teacher.

It's All in Your Head

You can see the changes happening to your body, but you can't see what's happening in your brain. Things are changing up there, too! As you grow up, your brain grows up, too. Along the way, you might feel moody or down in the dumps, or you might not like how you look. It helps to understand how puberty affects your emotions and your self-esteem.

Your Changing Brain

Becoming mature takes time for your body and your brain.

Brain Change

As you go from being a child to being a teenager, your body changes shape, you get taller, and you look different. Your brain changes a lot, too, developing and allowing you to master new skills. In a few years, you might play an instrument better than you ever imagined or read books that are filled with complicated words and ideas. You will become a better runner or artist or speaker or babysitter. Even if you do some of these things now, it takes time to become an expert, and this has a lot to do with the nerve fibers, called *neurons*, that fill your brain.

The more you study or practice something, the better you'll get. This is because repeating something—a vocabulary word or a piano piece or a basketball move—repeats the signal between two neurons. The more the neurons "talk," the stronger and faster their signal. As a result, you become a better student or musician or athlete.

Mostly Mature, but Not Quite

The word *mature* means fully grown and developed. During puberty, your body is changing and maturing, but you're not actually mature until you are a full-grown adult. The same is true for your brain.

One major brain change is happening in the front section of your brain, called the *frontal lobe*. This area will one day be the boss of the brain, in charge of helping you make good decisions. The problem is that the frontal lobe isn't fully developed yet—in fact, for most people it's not done maturing until their late teens or even early 20s. That doesn't mean you can't make good choices. Of course you can! But the part of your brain that makes the tough decisions quickly and on its own doesn't work perfectly just yet. Your parents can help you think about the risks of a decision in a way that your brain cannot quite do on its own.

Don't feel too frustrated—your brain is on its way to becoming fully mature. One day you will be able to think through a problem without asking for help. But since you are not there yet, let a parent, doctor, teacher, or other trusted adult help you when you are making a tough choice.

Moody You

"Grrr! Why do I feel this way?"

Emotional Roller Coaster

There probably isn't a girl on the planet who hasn't felt like whining, crying, or yelling at someone for no good reason. And if you don't like behaving this way, you're not alone. Most girls say they don't want to be moody but feel as though they can't control it. So what's going on?

The same hormones that affect your body during puberty also affect your brain. Hormone levels change constantly, rising and falling. This shifting and changing is important for your body's development, but it can make you feel grumpy. When your hormones swing, your moods can swing, too.

Manage Your Moods

Just because you feel a freak-out coming on doesn't mean you need to act on it. There are lots of ways to feel better without riding an emotional roller coaster.

Give yourself a time-out. Take a break when you feel frustration or anger coming on. Leave the room and get a little fresh air, or even just try taking a deep breath in and out and then counting to ten.

Take your anger out on something, not someone. Yelling at a person almost never helps (and often makes things worse), but the act of hollering or crying can feel like a relief. Screaming into a pillow makes it a lot quieter—and your pillow doesn't have any feelings for you to hurt!

Say you're sorry. Sometimes you just can't help your moods. If you know you've hurt or upset someone else, say you're sorry to help make the situation better and feel better about yourself.

Don't take it out on your body. If you are moody, don't make choices that will only cause you to feel worse. Try not to eat away your frustration, especially with junk food. And rather than lock yourself in your room, get outside! Fresh air almost always makes you feel better.

Get sleep. Being overtired can cause moods to swing, so try to get ten hours of good rest per night when you can.

Ditch the Drama
Since all girls your age are going through puberty and everyone is experiencing moodiness at random times, getting a group of girls together can lead to a lot of drama. If you see girls acting in a way you don't like, excuse yourself. Or don't join in the first place.

Stressed Out

Being stressed out can trigger even more moodiness. This stress often comes from outside stuff—an upcoming test, tryouts for a team, peer pressures, or family troubles—but your reaction to the stress is blown out of proportion by your hormones. Again, you may want to cry, scream, or throw a fit.

When you feel stress, your body feels it, too. And generally speaking, it's not a good feeling. Sometimes stress causes pain and other symptoms. You might have a bellyache or headache, or you might not be able to fall asleep at night. Even though stress is usually something in your head—a worry or a thought—you might feel it in the rest of your body.

Other times stress causes us to develop bad habits. Nail biting, under- or over-eating, and skin picking are some examples. Doing these things doesn't make you worry any less and just causes new problems. So try your best not to give in to bad habits when you are worried.

The best way to manage stress is to get rid of it. For instance, if you're worried about finishing a school project that you've been putting off, instead of panicking, just start working. If it isn't possible to ditch the stress, try these ideas to keep the stress from taking over:

Cut back. Lots of times, stress has to do with having too much going on. You may be able to handle each thing on its own, but when they are all jumbled together, things can feel overwhelming. Avoid this by making a schedule of what you can fit into your day, and get rid of distractions. And if you have a big performance or a test coming up, don't jump on the computer and waste time playing games.

Rest up. Sometimes the best defense against stress is a good night's sleep. When you are tired, you don't think clearly. So staying up extra late in order to finish something can backfire. Instead, you might be better off calling it a night and waking up early the next morning to finish.

Just breathe. Close your eyes and picture yourself relaxing. Just as the worries in your mind can cause stress in your body, by relaxing your mind you can make your body feel better, too.

You're Not Alone

One of the most important things to know is that you're not alone—no one likes the way it feels to be moody. Ask your mom if she remembers feeling this way when she was your age. Chances are, she will be able to tell you a story or two about life when she was going through puberty that will sound very familiar. Plus, your mom will be happy to hear that you're trying to take control of your moods.

Get Help!
There are times when your stress or moodiness may become severe, or you might have other feelings that seem overwhelming. You need to get help from a trusted adult and probably a doctor if you notice any of the following:

- You cannot sleep at night, several nights in a row.
- You cannot get out of bed in the morning, several mornings in a row.
- You find yourself crying constantly.
- You have lost your appetite and cannot eat.
- You have much less energy than you usually do, even for everyday routines.
- You feel as if you might hurt yourself or someone else.

Body Image

"Ugh! Why do I look this way?"

Look at You

As your body changes, it takes some getting used to. How you see your body and feel about what you see is called *body image*.

Sometimes a girl will look in the mirror and see herself as skinnier or heavier than she really is. This doesn't happen often, and most of the time all she needs is a little reassurance. If this happens to you, tell your mom or dad what you are worried about and ask them to be honest with you about how you look. If a misperception like this is severe or lasts a long time, health problems can follow, so you may need the extra help of a doctor or therapist.

Out of Control

When a girl becomes so focused on losing weight that she stops eating normally, she has an eating disorder. Living with this illness is very difficult. A girl's fierce desire to be thin can quickly spiral into dangerous habits and behaviors that she can't control. No matter how thin she becomes, she truly believes she is fat. Without help, she can become very sick. She can do permanent damage to her body, or even die. There are two main types of eating disorders: *anorexia* (an-uh-REX-ee-uh) and *bulimia* (buh-LEE-mee-uh).

Anorexia

Anorexia (the full name is *anorexia nervosa*) is an eating disorder that causes a girl to starve herself. A girl with anorexia intensely fears gaining weight. She becomes obsessed with ways to avoid food and often develops special rituals for eating in order to eat as little as possible. As she gets thinner and thinner, she will develop serious medical problems. She can even lose so much weight that she literally starves to death. A girl with anorexia might:

• refuse to eat, or eat only small amounts.
• eat only "safe" foods—those that are low in calories and fat.
• play with her food or cut it up to make it look eaten.
• weigh less than is healthy.
• express fear of gaining weight.
• exercise constantly.
• wear baggy clothes because she's convinced she doesn't look good
  in anything else or to hide the weight loss.

Bulimia

A girl who suffers from bulimia is also obsessed with being thin. But unlike a girl with anorexia, she doesn't starve herself to control her weight. Instead, she "binges" and then "purges." That means she eats a large amount of food in a short period of time and then tries to get rid of it by forcing herself to vomit, by using laxatives that cause her to go to the bathroom, or by exercising way more than normal. A girl who is bulimic may:

• become very secretive about food—about what, when, and how much
  she eats.
• save up or hide food.
• spend a lot of time thinking about and planning her next eating binge.
• take a lot of diet pills and laxatives.
• have stomach aches, a sore throat, or tooth decay from frequent vomiting.
• exercise much more than usual to try to burn off calories from food.

Getting Help

If you are struggling with an eating disorder, get help now. Don't let embarrassment force you to hide your problem. You have an illness that's not your fault. Talk to your parents or another adult you trust so that you can get the treatment you need. Don't suffer alone—this problem is too big for any girl to tackle by herself.

Like Yourself!

It's all about how you feel on the inside!

Self-Esteem

How you feel about yourself is called *self-esteem*. If you have high self-esteem, you think you are great; if it's low, you feel bad about yourself. Most people have a mix of the two: they feel positive about certain things (such as sports they play well and subjects in which they get good grades) and they feel negative about others (such as forgetting lines in a speech and how they look in comparison to other people).

Even though you can't possibly feel good about every little thing in your life, having good overall self-esteem is important. If you like who you are, other people will generally like you, too. But when you are going through puberty, this can be difficult. Your looks are changing, your moods are swinging, school is getting harder, and things you used to do just for fun—such as sports or music—might feel more competitive.

Feel Great!

High self-esteem doesn't always come automatically. There are some things you can do to help yourself feel good:

Positive talk: If you think and talk about what you like best about yourself, you will feel better in general. You will also present an image that makes others feel more positive about you. But be careful about how much positive talk you do out loud—you don't want to come off as being braggy.

Try new things: When you are feeling as if you aren't good at anything, it might be time to try something new. You may surprise yourself when you learn that you are actually very talented at something you have never tried before.

Stick with people who build you up: Surround yourself with friends who think you are great. It's no fun to be around people who say negative things, and this can make you feel bad about yourself, too.

Throw away the scale: One thing that can really rock a girl's self-esteem is normal weight gain. You cannot grow without gaining some weight! But still, at some point most girls worry that they are gaining too much or are not growing properly. Ditch the scale at home, and instead trust your parents and doctors to tell you how you are doing in this department.

Body Vibes

Even if you think you are hiding your feelings inside, your body language may be sharing how you feel with the rest of the world. Here are some ways that your body shows off how you feel about yourself.

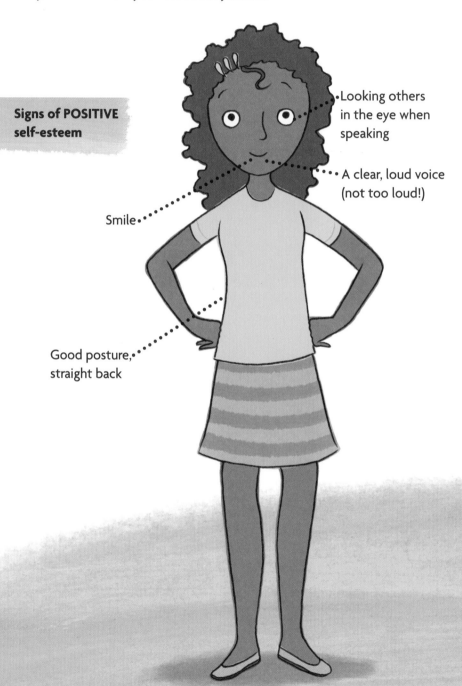

Signs of POSITIVE self-esteem

Looking others in the eye when speaking

A clear, loud voice (not too loud!)

Smile

Good posture, straight back

Looking away or down

Frown

A quiet, muffled voice

Slumped posture, curved shoulders

Signs of NEGATIVE self-esteem

Get Moving, Feel Better

Exercise your way toward a healthier and happier you.

Ready, Set, Move!

Exercise is not only great for your body; it's also great for your mind. You probably know the feeling of happiness after running around and playing outside with your friends. It's a kind of happiness that's hard to describe because you are exhausted from having so much fun. Hormones and other chemicals that are released when you exercise give your brain that wonderful feeling. Here are some basic exercise tips to keep you healthy and happy:

• Try to move your body enough so that you are huffing and puffing or sweating for at least 60 minutes every day.

• Get your exercise in different ways so that it doesn't become boring.

• If you don't have a chunk of time to set aside, exercise when you can throughout the day, because little bits of exercise add up.

• Take the tougher route, using the stairs instead of the elevator or riding your bike or walking instead of getting a ride. These are easy ways to add a little more exercise to your day.

Pair Up with a Parent

By exercising with a parent, you can do two things at once: you can work out and have alone time with your mom or dad. It's a win-win! Your parents need exercise, too, so they will be thrilled to do it with you. And it can be tough to find time to talk through things alone with a parent when brothers, sisters, and other friends and family get in the way. If you want time to ask a "growing-up" question, combine it with an activity such as a hike.

Get in a Group

There are lots of benefits to team sports:

• You can meet and have fun with other people.

• You can learn from more advanced players.

• Time usually passes pretty quickly when there's a game going on.

And don't forget that there are tons of group sports that don't require an official team. Just playing around in the yard inventing a game with a few friends can be a great way to exercise.

Don't Forget the Body Benefits

Remember that exercise is as important for your body as it is for your mind.

• It keeps you in shape.

• It strengthens your muscles and bones.

• It helps you sleep.

• It relieves stress.

Exercise DON'Ts

Don't push yourself so hard that you feel sick or that you hurt parts of your body.
Don't work out so hard that you cannot breathe! If you can't get a sentence out while you're exercising, you may be working your lungs too hard.
Don't try to do something that is too advanced for your level.
Don't exercise alone without supervision or in a place that's unfamiliar to you.
Don't try to exercise when you are sick—your body needs to heal, and that means rest, not working out.

Speak Up

When it comes to your body—and brain—it's best to talk through the tough stuff.

Talk Time

When something hurts your body, it is usually visible to others. Parents can see cuts, bruises, and rashes. You can describe headaches, growing pains, and cramps. But when you have emotional troubles, people might not notice unless you tell them. Feeling sad or angry isn't as obvious as having a fever. This is why it is important to talk things out.

As important as it is to share your feelings, carefully choosing who to talk to is even more critical. The best people to go to are the ones who care the most about you: your parents. You can also talk to teachers, doctors, and other trusted adults. All of these people can help you make good decisions, and they know when a problem is serious.

Your good friends are people you can go to in a bind. They will help you solve your problems, or at least they will try. But remember that friends your own age may not be able to give you the very best advice. While they can be excellent listeners, they might not be able to guide you as well as an adult.

Emotions Don't Fit in Bottles

Keeping your emotions locked inside isn't healthy. This creates stress, which—as you already know—can make you moody or interfere with sleep. Sometimes holding your feelings in makes them change: you might have started off sad or confused but after a while become angry or lonely.

By sharing your feelings with the right person, you can work through them or be reassured that everything is OK. And if it's not, by sharing your feelings you can begin to get help.

Help! Q&A

Girls just like you sent us their emotion-related questions. Here are the answers!

I get moody sometimes and get so mad so fast that I act weird. Sometimes I don't know who I am anymore. Help!
So Moody

As you grow up, it's perfectly normal to have major mood swings. Your body is changing, and your hormones affect the way you react to situations. It's also perfectly normal to be confused by the way you're feeling. One minute, you're only a little annoyed by something, and the next you're totally furious—it's hard to make sense of that. But it's great that you want to do something about your moodiness. Try to notice when it's about to happen so that you can get out of the situation and avoid a meltdown. Talk to your parents about what's going on with you so that they'll know exactly what you mean when you say, "I gotta go cool off."

I can't seem to stop worrying. Whether I'm worrying about my health, my family's health, or something in the news, I get a horrid feeling from it. I flip out every night! Help me settle down!
Need to Chill Out

A little bit of worry is OK—even healthy—but too much worry can be trouble. It sounds as if you are dealing with anxiety, which is a feeling of nervousness and worry that doesn't go away easily. Sometimes it's caused by the hormones in your body, and it's something that plenty of girls deal with. But anxiety gets in the way of you being happy and enjoying your life, and so it's important to learn how to reduce it. Describe how you're feeling to your parents and ask them to help you work on solving this issue with a counselor, therapist, or doctor. With a little help, you should start to feel better.

I don't feel pretty at all. All of my friends are beautiful and have boyfriends. I have been a tomboy all my life, and I'm starting to feel left out. Any advice?
Lonely

It's tough to feel that you don't fit in, and puberty can make you feel even more awkward. It's really easy to start comparing yourself to other girls. But remember this: beauty has nothing to do with whether a boy likes you. It isn't even what people see when they look at you. Real beauty is what you show with your words, your actions, and all your fun and cool qualities—including being a tomboy. Hang on tight to those things that make you different. After all, they're what make you you, and the people who will matter most to you are the ones who like you just the way you are—boys included.

Lately I've been having trouble liking myself and my personality. I've been trying to tell myself to love who I am, but I can't seem to do it. Do you know any ways that I can feel more proud of myself?
I Don't Like Me

It can be hard to feel good about yourself when you're in the middle of puberty. With your changing moods, your jam-packed days, and stress related to school, sports, activities, or responsibilities, you might behave in ways you don't like. That can make it hard to celebrate yourself. One solution is to make two lists: things you love about yourself and things you don't. Then make an effort to behave in the ways that show up in the positive list and not in the negative one. Along the way, give yourself a break. Life can be a challenge sometimes, and it's really true that you don't have to be perfect.

Your Body, Your World

As you go through puberty, you might relate to your family and friends differently. How should you present yourself so that people treat you as if you are older— but not too old? As you get more mature, you will gain your own style, get used to your new body, and develop confidence about your place in the world around you.

Family Dynamics

Spend time with your family for a well-balanced you.

Family Time

A lot of things may change when you go through puberty. You may feel more private and want to have more alone time. Or your interests may change, leaving you wanting to spend more time with just your friends.

Either way, spending time with your family is really important, because these are the people who will be around you to support you for the rest of your life! Many parents will set aside regular family times, such as Sunday night dinners. While this may seem to interfere with your social life, it is often the only way that everyone in the family (not just you) can make time to spend with one another.

To keep your family bonds strong as you go through puberty, make sure to invest time in those relationships. Now that you are getting older, you need to carve out time from your busy schedule for your parents and siblings. Here are some easy ways to keep close family ties every day of the week.

Walk and Talk Monday: Take an evening walk together around the neighborhood, changing routes each week.

Book Club Tuesday: Each family member shares a favorite book or maybe everyone reads the same book and talks about it.

Top It Off Wednesday: Throw a family pizza party for dinner, where each person gets to make his or her own individual pizza with the exact toppings he or she loves.

Catch Up Thursday: Play different games of catch, switching from a softball to a baseball to a flying disc from week to week.

Friday Fun Night: Gather the gang together for a night of games. Try board games one week and relay races the next.

Give Back Saturday: As a family, decide where your help is needed in the community, and then volunteer your time for a couple of hours each weekend.

Sunday Morning Rise and Shine: Work together to make a creative breakfast everyone can enjoy.

The Sibling Situation

One day, you feel as if your sibling is your very best friend. But the next day, he seems like a baby. You don't want to watch the same shows anymore, you aren't interested in his games, and he just seems immature. Sound familiar?

As your body changes, it's not uncommon to feel as if you are outgrowing your siblings. You are changing pretty quickly and, well, they aren't. If you have older brothers or sisters, they might have felt the same way about you—when they went through puberty, you seemed young and silly to them.

This is entirely normal. And one day, you and your siblings will all be adults, so you will all feel the same age again. But during this particular time, as your body and brain are changing, so are your interests. Even though you might feel as if you are outgrowing a younger brother or sister, try to include him or her when you can. Your sibling will really appreciate it . . . and it can be fun for you to just be a "kid" for a while.

Oh, Brother . . . or Sister

One of the most embarrassing situations can occur when your sibling shares highly private information about you. Families talk about many different things, and some of them are meant to be kept inside the family. So when your personal news gets spread all over school—especially information about your body or your feelings—it can be humiliating.

Often, brothers or sisters will share something because they didn't realize it was supposed to be kept private. So if you want a piece of information to stay within the family, tell your family that.

Sometimes a sibling will spread information on purpose, knowing you will be upset. That's not OK, and you need to talk it through—possibly with help from a parent—so that it doesn't happen again.

Don't forget that respecting privacy works both ways. If your sibling wants something kept secret, don't blab it around to others!

Your Social Circle

Good friends will stand by your side through good times and bad times—and puberty.

Support Circle

There's an old saying that "birds of a feather flock together." You and your friends are all going through puberty at the same time. You know how your friends feel, and together you can form a great support circle. Your flock can help one another through tough times, and by sticking together you'll see that the changes in your body and your emotions are pretty common.

Good Advice?

When reaching out to a friend about puberty or your body, it's hard to know how much advice you should take from a person your age. Some girls know a lot about body development and general health. Even so, it's better to turn to an adult. Your friend may know lots about one particular issue, but while the information might be correct, it could just be specific to her own situation. This doesn't mean you can't ask for her advice, but it's always best to get an opinion from someone who really knows!

Not-So-Safe Secrets

Whether you're asking questions or just comparing what you're each going through, talking about your body is a very personal thing. Just as when you choose to share a secret, it's important to trust the person you tell about your body. A good rule of thumb is to keep your lips zipped unless you wouldn't care if your secret slipped out.

The same is true when it comes to technology. Whether you're e-mailing, texting, IMing, or posting to a website, whatever you put out there about yourself is available for others to see. This means that if you share personal information—such as your address or phone number—other people can get it.

And that goes for pictures, too. Post a picture online or send one to a friend's e-mail inbox, and it could be seen by her family members, printed and passed around school, forwarded to an e-mail address list, and posted on other sites. Before you know it, your picture could wind up being viewed by all sorts of strangers. You might have thought the photo was funny when you sent it, but later you could have regrets because the picture was inappropriate and now you can't take it back.

On the Receiving End

What about the private information your friends share with you? It can become difficult to know when you should keep something to yourself and when you should share it. If a friend asks you to guard a secret and not to tell anyone, most of the time you should respect her request and keep the information to yourself.

Still, there may be times when you need to tell someone because your friend is in danger. Some examples include her

• cutting her skin.

• avoiding eating or throwing up after eating.

• feeling so sad she might harm herself.

• being touched, hit, or even spoken to in an abusive way.

In any of these situations, your friend needs help from an adult. It can feel awful to break her confidence, but if you are ever unsure and you think that a secret might hurt your friend or someone else, that's a secret to share. Tell a trusted adult, such as a parent. Remember, it's your parents' job to keep you safe and healthy, and they can help do the same for your friends. Your mom or dad can then help you to decide whether a secret can stay quiet. Even if your friend says she doesn't want anyone to know, she will thank you later for helping her.

Pressures and Rules

Keep your body and mind strong by saying no to bad choices.

The Good and the Bad

Your friends can have a big influence on the decisions you make, from where you sit for lunch to what you talk about, and from the clothes you wear to the hobbies you do. It's called *peer pressure*. Peer pressure isn't the same as bullying or forcing. In fact, peer pressure isn't even always negative. You may have experienced positive peer pressure in gym class if you were motivated to run a mile because someone else in class could do it. Or maybe you signed up for a study group because a friend said that it helped her improve her spelling.

But then there's the bad. Negative peer pressure occurs when you make bad choices just so that you can fit in with your so-called friends. Some examples are

- cutting class or skipping school.
- gossiping about or bullying another person.
- swearing or talking back.
- drinking, smoking, or taking drugs.
- wearing clothing or makeup that your parents feel is inappropriate.
- piercing or permanently changing your body in any way without permission.
- watching movies or television shows that your parents disapprove of.
- stealing or vandalizing.

Your job is to keep your body healthy and safe. So get comfortable with saying no. A real friend won't push you and will respect your decision. She may even listen to why you're not participating. Your "no" could help someone else make better choices, too (positive peer pressure!).

If a friend is giving you too much negative pressure, then she's a friend to walk away from. This can be a very tough thing to do. But remember that your body is the only one you'll ever have, so you need to treat it right. If your friend doesn't respect your decisions, she's not worth keeping around.

Different Rules for Different Houses

Peer pressure gets a little trickier when it comes to spending time at your friends' homes. Rules vary from house to house. Some parents may allow sweets while others stock only fruits and veggies. Some parents have different rules about what TV shows their kids can watch or how long they are allowed to sit in front of a computer screen. In some houses, video games are OK. In other houses, they're not. And in some it depends upon the content of the game.

Whether you agree with these rules or not, they are the rules. And your parents are in charge of your rules. Your rules exist whether you are at home or out and about. If you break those rules just because the limits are different at a friend's house, you will still face consequences when you get home. If you are at a friend's house and she is allowed to do something you are not, check in with your parents first.

It can feel unfair that some kids have different rules—you may think that the situation at another house is less strict and more fun. Rather than fighting with your parents or breaking the rules, ask them why they have chosen certain limits. You may be able to change some of your parents' rules, and, if not, at least you will understand why the rules are there in the first place.

Regardless of the rules, some friends will say that they are allowed to do some things that they are really *not* allowed to do. For instance, your friend may tell you that she is allowed to go out without an adult's supervision or that she can eat whatever she wants whenever she wants. Things that sound suspicious are probably untrue, and they could also be dangerous. So even if your friend swears that she's allowed to do something, if it doesn't sound like a good idea, don't join her.

Taking Your Body into Your Own Hands

Think through your choices before making changes to your body.

Temporary Changes

There are lots of things you cannot control about the way your body changes during puberty: the size of your breasts, how tall you will ultimately become, how much hair grows on your legs, or when you'll get your period for the very first time.

When you feel as though your body is taking over, you may want to react by taking back control. You may be tempted to make some temporary changes that can alter your looks just a little bit, such as

• putting on makeup.
• painting your nails.
• coloring your hair.
• wearing heels.
• shaving your legs.

But even though these changes are temporary, you shouldn't actually do any of them without talking to your parents first! Even if nail polish can be removed or heels can go back into the closet, parents have strong feelings about how you present yourself to the world.

For instance, some moms are OK with makeup, some say "absolutely not," and some are comfortable when their daughters use makeup to cover up acne but don't want them wearing lipstick or eye shadow yet. Your parents' rules RULE, so ask before you do anything to alter your appearance.

Play It Safe

A little temporary change may not seem like a big deal. But in reality, some of these fixes can have dangers.

Nails: Since lots of people get manicures and pedicures at nail salons, it's easy for germs to spread—and for you to get an infection—if the salon doesn't properly clean and sterilize the equipment. Before going to any salon, make sure a parent gives the OK first. And if you walk in but it seems unclean, walk out!

Hair: If you've ever thought about getting highlights or dyeing your hair, you might want to think again. There is a lot of debate over the hazards of chemicals in hair dye, and some people think changing your hair color could be a health risk. Some people are also allergic to hair dye, so they wind up with an itchy, burning scalp—or worse!

Henna tattoos: These tattoos last several days (sometimes a couple of weeks), and they eventually fade away. The problem occurs when you are allergic to the ingredients in the product. Because the tattoo stays on for so long, if you have an allergic reaction, your skin will be red, irritated, and itchy as long as the tattoo lasts.

Tanning: Whether you lie out in the sun or check into a tanning salon for a little extra glow, the rays are definitely harmful to you. These rays can lead to wrinkles, age spots, and even skin cancer later in life! Skip the tanning salon and always wear sunscreen (at least 30 SPF) when you go out.

Permanent Changes

Just as there are ways to temporarily change how you look, there are ways to permanently alter yourself as well. Doing something that forever changes your body is a big deal and should never happen without a parent's permission.

A good example of a permanent change is ear piercing. Once a hole is poked through your skin, the hole is there for good—or if you take the piercing out after just a short time, a scar will remain in its place. Either way, you will have a mark. If you get your ears pierced by someone who doesn't know what she is doing, you could wind up with very lopsided piercings—or worse, an infection.

When your ear is pierced, a sharp needle goes through the skin of the earlobe and pokes through to the other side. If the needle isn't *sterile* (if it hasn't been properly cleaned to make sure it is free of bacteria), your ear can become red, swollen, and infected. The earring must come out, and you may even need medicine.

After piercing your ears, you have to take good care of your lobes. Otherwise, the skin on the earlobe can get irritated or it can even grow over the earring backing. Because it takes so much effort to make sure a piercing heals well, and because piercing is permanent, you really need the help of a parent with this decision.

Changing Body, Changing Style

Make good fashion choices for your new body to let your personal style shine through.

Set Your Style

Another way to control how you look is through the clothes that you wear. As you get older, you get to choose from a much wider range of clothes, shoes, products, and accessories. You will play with lots of different looks, and eventually you will find your style.

It is important to respect your body. Your body is yours—it doesn't have to be shared with the world. And style can be cute and sophisticated without showing off too much. Most parents have rules about what clothes are appropriate. You can find a great look while still respecting your parents' limits.

Unwanted Attention

You might notice that as your body changes, you start getting attention from other people. Sometimes siblings make fun, but this is usually because they don't know what else to say. If you don't like it, let them know how you feel. If you are getting unwanted attention from your peers or strangers, talk to your parents about how best to handle the uncomfortable situations.

Size Is Just a Number

What size am I? This sounds like a simple question, but it can be complicated because there is no standard for sizing. So you may be a girls' size 14 in one store and a women's size 4 in another. Or you might fit into a medium pant but a large shirt in the same store. Figuring out your size can be very confusing, mostly because different clothing manufacturers use slightly different size guidelines.

Choosing a larger or smaller size than you usually wear may affect the way you feel, but you shouldn't let a number or a size make a difference to your self-esteem. One way to manage this is to avoid reading so much into sizes. Choose clothes that fit well, regardless of the size number. If you're comfortable in an outfit that fits you right, you will look and feel great; who cares what the tag says? After all, no one ever sees that tag except you.

False Photos

Just about everywhere you look, there are pictures of perfect-looking people—smiling in advertisements, acting in movies, and modeling clothes. It's easy to forget that those images aren't just snapshots. The pictures in magazines, on TV, in movies, and online show people who have been made up to look a certain way. And then the image is often changed (using computer retouching) so that a person will look even thinner or younger. These pictures are not good role models. Pick real people whose look and style you admire, because the way actors and models look in glossy pictures isn't how they look in real life!

Help! Q&A

Girls just like you sent us their questions about fitting into the world around them. Here are the answers!

I am only 12 years old, but my friends seem to want to grow up so fast! I don't want to grow up. I just want to stay a kid forever, but I feel pressured into being a teen. What should I do?
Just a Kid

Take your time! Once you grow up, you're a grown-up forever, so enjoy being a kid for as long as you can. That doesn't mean that you won't need to grow up a little—you'll have new responsibilities and expectations every year. But there's no rush to look or act older than you are. If your friends start making decisions that make you uncomfortable, don't feel as if you need to go along with them. And if you're not sure what to do, talk it through with your parents. They can help you make choices that are right for you.

I'm a very social person, and being with my friends is a big deal to me. Most of the time I would rather be spending the night at my friend's house or e-mailing someone than spending time with my family. My relationship with the people who REALLY matter is falling apart, yet friends still seem so important! Have any advice?
Friends Forever

Lots of girls face this problem. It's normal to want to spend time with your friends because hanging out with them is part of becoming independent and, well, because you really like them. But your family members are going to be in your life always, and it's important to give them the same time and respect that you give to your friends. So find a balance. Schedule regular time to spend with your family, and enjoy yourself while you are with them. That way, you'll feel connected to your friends *and* your family, which will make you a happier girl.

I'm shorter and smaller than all of my friends, and they sometimes treat me like a baby. But I'm not a baby—I'm the second oldest of our group! How do I get them to treat me like an equal?
Shorty

Speak up! This could be one of those situations where friends think they're making jokes but actually they are hurting your feelings. Next time a friend treats you like a baby, say, "Hey, being small is not the same as being young. I feel bad when you say that." That should help your friends to see that they should cut it out. But you can't control how other people act—including people who don't even know you but treat you like a little kid just because of your size. The best thing to do is to respond maturely: "Actually, I'm 11, so I can handle this by myself. But thanks for your help."

My friends are all starting to wear makeup, but my mom will only let me wear lip gloss. My friends say I should just wear makeup when I'm at school and then wash it off before I go home, but I'm afraid of getting into trouble. Help!
Bare Skin

First things first—you don't need to wear makeup just because your friends say you should. But if you'd like to try it, talk to your mom. She can explain why she thinks makeup isn't right for you, and you might be able to find a compromise. But even if you don't agree, your mom's rules RULE, and that means you need to follow them even when you aren't home. It would be awful if your mom found out that you were breaking her trust by wearing makeup anyway. And if your friends keep giving you a hard time, you can tell them the truth—that a little makeup is just not worth getting into big trouble for.

Love the Skin You're In

You're fabulous just the way you are!

It's All About You!

The most important fact about puberty is that it is different for everyone. Each girl's body will develop in its own way, on its own schedule. There is no perfect shape to strive for.

There is also no perfect time for puberty. In fact, most girls would say there is no good time. The girls whose bodies change first often feel embarrassed about that. But so do the girls whose bodies change last. And guess what? The girls who are going through changes right in the middle—they usually feel funny, too!

Perhaps the hardest part of all of this is getting used to the new person you see in the mirror. You will change in noticeable ways. Every girl has at least one moment (and often more!) when she looks at herself and doesn't like what she sees. That's OK, but talk about it with a trusted adult. If you and your parents decide you need to make changes, work on these changes together—you will feel supported, and you are much more likely to succeed.

It's completely normal to struggle with the new you. Eventually, you will learn to love the skin you're in. For now, look for things about your body that you like— even love! You can't rush this journey, so enjoy being your age. And along the way to adulthood, never forget to celebrate you!

Glossary

When puberty and body changes come into play, a lot of new words will be thrown your way. Here's what they mean.

acne: inflammation of the skin that causes red, black, or white bumps; these bumps are also known as pimples, zits, whiteheads, and blackheads.

anemia: lower-than-normal number of red blood cells in the blood.

anorexia nervosa: an eating disorder characterized by limited food intake or refusal to eat food because of fear of becoming overweight.

areola: the red or darkened area around the nipple of the breast.

body image: a person's perception of how she looks; how a person sees her own body.

body mass index (BMI): an equation calculated by a doctor that relates height to weight; BMI helps determine whether a person weighs too much, too little, or the right amount given how tall she is.

breast buds: the first bumps to appear where the breasts will grow; these are underneath the nipple and are about the size of a small stack of nickels.

bulimia: an eating disorder characterized by eating large amounts of food in a short period of time (called bingeing) followed by trying to get rid of the food calories through vomiting, laxative use, or excessive exercise (called purging).

calcium: a mineral stored in the body, mostly in the bones and teeth; people get their calcium through foods, drinks, and sometimes multivitamins or mineral supplements.

cramp: a pain associated with having a period (usually a dull squeezing or twisting sensation, though sometimes sharp) anywhere between the bottom of your ribcage and the top of your hips.

depilatory: a chemical used for hair removal.

estrogen: a hormone made in the ovaries and responsible for many of the changes in a young woman's body, including breast development; once a girl gets her period, estrogen is responsible for building the uterine lining and helping to regulate the menstrual cycle.

fallopian tubes: the tubes (one on each side) that lead from each ovary to the uterus.

flow: a word used to describe the bleeding during a period—this term is a little misleading because the blood does not "flow" like a stream.

folliculitis: inflammation or infection of hair follicles in the skin.

frontal lobe: part of the brain located in the front, behind the forehead; this area is in charge of decision making, problem solving, and many other functions and is one of the last parts of the brain to mature.

FSH: short for follicle-stimulating hormone, a hormone released by the brain that tells an egg in one of the ovaries to mature.

growing pains: discomfort associated with getting taller—sometimes these pains are caused by stretching bones, muscles, or ligaments, but most of the time they are related to running, jumping, or other activities.

growth hormone: the hormone released by your brain that tells your body to grow.

hormones: chemicals naturally produced by the body that tell organs what to do.

ingrown hairs: hairs that get caught underneath the skin while trying to grow; these hairs can curl back or grow sideways, and when they do, they cause bumps under the skin.

insulin: the hormone that helps sugar get out of the blood and into cells so that it can be used for energy.

keratosis pilaris: very small skin-colored bumps that make the skin feel rough; they often appear on the backs of the arms but can also be on the cheeks, chest, or legs.

labia: the skin folds outside the vagina.

LH: short for luteinizing hormone, a hormone released by the brain that tells an egg in one of your ovaries to release itself (ovulation).

mature: to become fully grown and developed.

menarche: another name for the first time you get your period.

menstrual cycle: the events (shifting hormones, release of the egg, and shedding of the uterine lining) that happen from the start of one period to the start of another.

menstrual period: the release of blood when the lining of the uterus is shed; also known as "period."

menstruate: another term for having your period.

middleschmirtz: sometimes called "ovulation pain"; this is a feeling some girls get when the egg is about to be released from the ovary in the middle of a menstrual cycle.

mid-parental target height: the math equation that estimates a child's adult height based upon her parents' heights.

neuron: a type of cell that carries messages from one part of the body to another; your brain is made mostly of neurons, and they help you think and act.

nipple: part of the breast that sticks up in the middle.

Osgood Schlatter: a painful bump on the upper shinbone, just below the knee.

ovaries: the female reproductive glands located in the lower abdomen (near your hips) and containing unfertilized eggs.

ovulation: the release of an egg from one ovary.

pad: a specially packaged tissue that fits inside the underpants and absorbs menstrual fluid.

papilla: the medical name for nipple.

peer pressure: the influence (both good and bad) that friends have upon choices.

period: the release of blood when the lining of the uterus is shed; also known as "menstrual period."

pore: a tiny opening in the skin that allows sweat to come out onto the skin surface; pores can also clog, causing acne.

progesterone: a hormone, made in the ovaries, that is involved in regulating the menstrual cycle.

protein: an essential nutrient that provides energy to the body and is required by all of the body's cells.

puberty: the time during which the body matures and develops; in girls, puberty includes the development of breasts and pubic hair, body odor, and ultimately menstruation.

pubic area: the area just above the genital organs.

pubic hair: hair on the external genital organs.

self-esteem: how a person feels about herself.

spotting: when little drops of blood or uterine tissue come out of the vagina—this can happen toward the end of a period, or it can happen at another point in the cycle when a girl is not having her period.

swelling: when a part of the body looks or feels a little bit bigger, usually because it contains some extra water or blood.

tampon: a specially packaged tissue that fits inside the vagina and soaks up blood during a period.

toxic shock syndrome (TSS): a very serious and very rare infection caused by bacteria; toxic shock can result from leaving a tampon in too long and from other causes as well.

trusted adult: an adult you can talk to about private and sensitive issues; trusted adults can include parents, older siblings, relatives (grandparents, aunts), doctors, coaches, and teachers.

ureters: the tubes that carry urine from the kidneys to the bladder.

urethra: the tube that leads from the bladder out of the body—this is where urine (pee) comes out, and it is located just in front of the vagina.

urinary tract: the path of urine (or pee)—this tract starts at the kidneys where urine is made, goes down the ureters, into the bladder, and then out the urethra.

UTI: short for urinary tract infection, an infection caused by bacteria growing somewhere along the urinary tract.

vagina: the part of the body between the uterus and the labia; the vagina is where blood flows out during a period, but it is not where urine (pee) comes out.

vaginal discharge: a clear or whitish fluid that comes out of the vagina; it often has the consistency of mucus.

yeast infection: a common type of vaginal infection caused by a fungus (yeast).

Still don't see something you want to know about? Check with a parent, doctor, coach, or other trusted adult. Good info is always important!

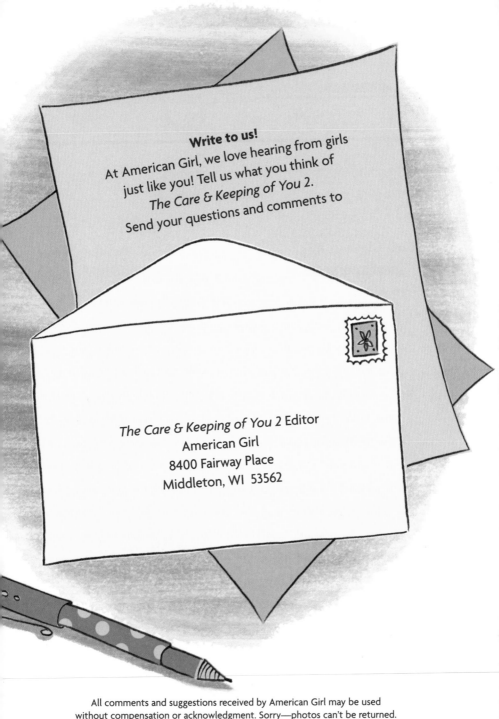

Write to us!
At American Girl, we love hearing from girls just like you! Tell us what you think of *The Care & Keeping of You 2.* Send your questions and comments to

The Care & Keeping of You 2 Editor
American Girl
8400 Fairway Place
Middleton, WI 53562

All comments and suggestions received by American Girl may be used without compensation or acknowledgment. Sorry—photos can't be returned.

Here are some other American Girl books you might like:

❑ I read it.

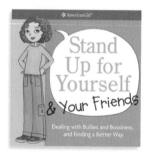

❑ I read it.

❑ I read it.

❑ I read it.

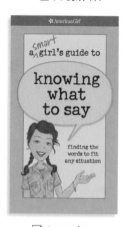

❑ I read it.

❑ I read it.